Bev and Lee,

This book made me think
of the two of you who are such
role models for all of us on
how love can endure as you
have proven with your 50th
anniversary.

Mazel Tove!

Love,
Lois

*M*y love for you is not a gift
To you
It is a gift
To me

— Leonard Nimoy

For Susan

people we love
and strangers too
are shedding tears
and walking
sad and dusty streets

your hand touches mine
and comforts me

love is the beginning
and the end

A Lifetime *of*
LOVE

Poems on the Passages of Life

Leonard
Nimoy

Blue Mountain Press™
SPS Studios, Inc., Boulder, Colorado

Library of Congress Catalog Card Number: 2001007263
ISBN: 0-88396-596-8

Certain trademarks are used under license.

Manufactured in China
First Printing: March 2002

 This book is printed on recycled paper.

This book is printed on fine quality, laid embossed, 80 lb. paper. This paper has been specially produced to be acid free (neutral pH) and contains no groundwood or unbleached pulp. It conforms with all the requirements of the American National Standards Institute, Inc., so as to ensure that this book will last and be enjoyed by future generations.

Library of Congress Cataloging-in-Publication Data

Nimoy, Leonard.
  A lifetime of love : poems on the passages of life / Leonard Nimoy.
    p. cm.
  ISBN 0-88396-596-8 (hardcover : alk. paper)
  I. Title.
  PS3564.I5 L64 2002
  811'.54—dc21

                                        2001007263
                                        CIP

SPS Studios, Inc.
P.O. Box 4549, Boulder, Colorado 80306

Contents

Introduction

*W*hen I was a very young boy, perhaps eight or nine years old, and had not yet learned to swim, my mother took me to a beach on a hot summer day. It was walking distance, about twenty minutes from our home in Boston.

From a concrete upper level where my mother laid out towels, one could walk down a short flight of steps to the sand and water. We had been here before, and I was capable of working my way down and playing at the water's edge while Mom rested upstairs. But on this particular day, the tide was in and the water had risen onto the steps. The sandy strip of beach was covered. Thinking that I could stand waist deep in the water, I stepped off the concrete stairs and immediately found myself in water over my head. I could see the stairs from under the water and I desperately reached out, but a slight surge took me away and the stairs were inches beyond my reach.

In a panic I kicked and thrashed, drinking seawater. I was able, once or twice, to kick off the bottom, but could not get hold of the steps which were so agonizingly close.

One time I even managed to grab the arm of a boy who was standing on the bottom step, but he, thinking I was being playfully aggressive, shouted "let go" and shook me loose back into the water. I was desperate and losing my last bit of strength when suddenly I felt a hand grasp my wrist and pull me up onto the concrete step. It was a teenage girl who evidently had seen my struggle and decided I needed help.

The water was pouring from my nose and mouth as I stood next to her and managed to say, "Thank you very much." Then she dove into the water, and I made my way upstairs and lay down in the sun next to my mother. Not wanting to alarm her, I never said a word about the event. Still, I consider to this day, that my life was saved by someone who reached out a hand in a moment of caring. It was my first such rescue, but not my last.

A Lifetime of Love

I am an incurable romantic
I believe in hope, dreams and decency

    I believe in love
    Tenderness and kindness

I believe in mankind

    I believe in goodness
    Mercy and charity
    I believe in a universal spirit
    I believe in casting bread
    Upon the waters

        I am awed by the snow-capped mountains
        By the vastness of the oceans

        I am moved by a couple
        Of any age — holding hands
        As they walk through city streets

A living creature in pain
Makes me shudder with sorrow
A seagull's cry fills me
With a sense of mystery

A river or stream
Can move me to tears
A lake nestling in a valley
Can bring me peace

I am still a child

Thrilled by a sunrise
Touched by a bird-song
Delighted by a clown

Frightened by hatred
Hurt by rejection
Saddened by pain

Warmed by a lifetime of love

On a soft Sunday afternoon
We drifted into
The concert hall, small
The audience sparse
Hushed and waiting

Why? How did we come
To be here? I don't recall
Perhaps a tiny notice, a newspaper
A flier, a poster on a bookstore wall

The houselights dimmed
And they arrived, two artists
Asian women, I recall
A cello and a violin, and they began

And we in tandem reached
And found each other's hand
And held and were loving

And something in the music
What did they play?
It touched our love and stroked it
And filled our hearts so full
That it spilled into our eyes
And in the dark we both reached
To touch away the wet of love
On each other's cheeks

And it was a soft, soft
Sunday
A soft Sunday afternoon

I have seen
   The beauty of love
      In your face

I have met
   The joy of existence
      In your being

I have found
   The eternity of life
      In your presence

I have touched
   The fulfillment
      Of perpetual grace

      And it is you
      All of it
         Is you

*W*hatever we are
   We belong together

Wherever we are
   We will find each other

Whoever we are
   We are
      Forever one

$\mathcal{M}$y love is a garden

You are the sun

When you shine
On my garden
It grows

You feed it
With your smile

You warm it
With your heart

You bless it
With your being

When friends say
My, you have a
Beautiful garden

I look at you
And smile

*B*lessed is the morning sun
That lights
Your smiling eyes

Blessed are your shining eyes
That touch
My warming heart

Blessed is my joyous heart
That beats
Within your love

*T*he miracle is this...
The more we share
The more
We have

*A*fter endless days
Of highest flight

Sunny days
Of dizzy heights

I found myself
Suddenly
On the ground
Weighted down

Lost
And searching
For the light

And then
I saw you shine
Clear and sweet

And I took
Your outstretched hand

And found my way
To joyous love
And dream-filled days

You led me home

*Y*ou stepped
   Deep into
      The waters
      Of my soul

Patiently you searched
   For the precious
         Stone

You found it
   Warmed it
      Caressed it
And gave it
   To me
Unselfishly
   As a gift

And now
   It is ours
      And we call it
         Love

Only You

*H*iding underground
Disguised by success
My pain began in seed
Nurtured in the dark
And growing, swelling
Into life

It breathed
Deep and strong
Until it stood
As tall as me
And growing still
Casting a shadow
To block the sun
And chilling me
With fright

And only you
Could see and know
And only you could stand
Eye to eye
And face my dragon down
And hold out the sword to me
With which to do the slaying
And the dragon fell

And the two of us
Dragonslayers
Who have found tomorrow
Are left standing
In the bright of light

You are the dream
    I dream

You are the sun
    I seek

You are
    My shade

You are the rest
    I sleep

You are the peace
    I yearn for

You are
    My hope
        My love

*L*ove does happen
    Like a touch
        Of grace

It falls
Into place
Where there used
    To be
        Empty space

When I hold your
        Face
In my hands
        I ask
How did this happen
        To me?

Because I Care
About You

*T*hese words are for you
To have
  To hold
    To keep from now on
      Forever

        I love you
        Need you
        I need your laughter
        I need your love
        Need your warmth

        Because
          I care about you
            And
              I love you

*W*hen I see
The sorrows of the world
  Leaning heavy
    On your shoulders
  I wish they were
    On mine instead

        Because
          I care about you

I want to shout it in the streets

Wake up!   Life is here!   Live it!

Listen to the music
The rhapsody, the symphony
That surrounds you

Yet each must find it
In his or her own way
In their own time
The awakening, the blossoming

Those who find it are blessed
They carry a special aura
A look of beauty and insight
Peace and wisdom

I like myself…
Because of you

*S*o many times
I've thought…

   I need
      I want
         Someone to help me

   Someone to understand
      To care

   Someone or something
      To soothe this emptiness
      This feeling of being lost

It never works that way

   When I care
   When I help or console
   Or offer understanding
      To someone else

   My own emptiness disappears
   And I am fulfilled

I don't touch you often enough
   I don't tell you often enough
   That I care about you

*L*et me not take for granted
   An act of kindness
   An offering of love
   The glory of human courage
   A sign of respect
   A phrase of beautiful music
   A decent soul
   The beauty of a blossom
   And above all
         You

A Time to Give

It is time
     to give
For I have been given
          so much

And now it is time
          to give in return

I have seen pleasure
          and sorrow
          triumph
               and defeat

I have seen
          the joys of life
          and watched
          the face of death

I have walked
          the road
Which sometimes seemed
          unbearably long
          hard and unbending

I have seen it
          suddenly become
               a path of glory
               rich
                    fertile
                    lush
                         and giving

*W*hatever I have passed on
　　has come back
　　　　to me
　　　　　　in word
　　　　　　　　and deed

Whatever I have given
　　I have gained

And now
　　I shall
　　　　start the cycle
　　　　　　again

*W*hen you
　　let me take
　　　　I'm grateful

When you
　　let me give
　　　　I'm blessed

*D*ay after day
    passes
As I wonder
    what next?
What shall I do next?

What shall I begin
    to try
    to do
    to challenge
      myself?

Finally
    the answer comes
      simply…
        clearly…

Do something
    for someone else…
Some surprise
    something…
Some unexpected
    something
    which says
    I thought
      of you
    I care
      about you
    I wanted
      to do
        something
          for you

*T*ake these words
    for they are yours

Take these thoughts
    for what else
    can I give?

What more can I give
Than the thought
    that you are
      loved

Take this love
    for who else
Could I give it to
      but you

I know
That there is nothing
    in this world
That you wouldn't do
    if I asked you to
And I would do
The same for you

I'm not always able to give

I'm sometimes empty

And even when
    I want to give
    Sometimes I can't find
    The key to the door of me

And even when I get
    The door open
        Sometimes
        There's nothing there

So please understand
    When I can't give

In a little time
    I'll be full again

I love to give
    And as soon
        As I can
        I will

Help me...

Help me
To say I love you
Because I do

It should be easy
To say I love you
Because
It's true

What is this fear
That ties my tongue
That locks
The words
Away inside
Deep inside?

Help me
Turn the key

Help me
To speak
The truth...

Help me to say
I love you

I came to you
    lonely and
       drifting…

You taught me
    what I'm worth

I came to you
    hungry
       and I was fed

I came to you
    needing
       and you gave

When I talked
    when I spoke
    of my yearnings
       and my dreams…
You listened
    and not only listened
       you heard

          Will you let me
              do
           the same
           for you?

*I*f the sun turns cold

If the night is too dark
　long and lonely

Try me

If your trust
　has been betrayed

If dreams won't
　come true

When hopes seem
　to crumble
　and fade
　　to dust

Try me

If your sadness
　leaves a void

An emptiness
　which can't
　　be filled
　except
　by love

Try me

We Are All Children Searching for Love

I am convinced
That if all mankind
Could only gather together
In one circle
Arms on each other's shoulders
And dance, laugh and cry
    Together
   Then much
      Of the tension and burden
       Of life
     Would fall away
In the knowledge that
We are all children

Needing and wanting
Each other's
Comfort and
Understanding

We are all children
Searching for love

We are all children
    Seeking the fountain
We are all children
    Washed by the rain

We are the dreamers
    We are the dancers

Life is the music
    Love is the song

We are all children
Needing laughter
Fighting tears
    Hiding fears

We are all children
Seeking release
Hungry for peace…

We are all children
Crossing the ocean
We are all children
Tossed by the storm

Swimming the waters
Of God's devotion
Seeking a harbor to
Offer us home

We are all children
Of various ages

We are all children
The near and the far

Give us the peace
To search not for sages
Give us the strength
To love what we are

*C*ome
    Let us dance together
      Sing together

Let us reawaken
    The innocence
    The wonder
    The simple
    Joy and faith
Which is rightfully ours

Let us unburden ourselves
    Of the disguises
      The roles
      The weights
      The chains...
Which hide and bind
The children
    That we are

For we are
    All of us —
      Children

You and I

In my heart
Is the seed of the tree
Which will be me

Nourished by understanding
Warmed by friends
Fed by loved ones
Matured by wisdom
Tempered by tears…

Searching for me

I wander
Through a house of mirrors

I see a myriad of images
But none are mine

Only distorted reflections
Of a stranger

Someone I've met
But don't really know

I cry out my name
But the hollow echo that responds
Tells me I must wait

It is not yet time

And then…
One day in the spring of my life
The buds and the blossoms appear

I am alive

I am here

I have joined the earth
Like a tide pool…
Filled by the mist
And the great waves
Giving of myself
To the air and the earth
Living at peace
With the sun and moon
Cousin to the fog and rain

The melody is simple

And the words are sweet

I am
I am ready
I am ready to give
I am ready to give and to receive
I am ready to give and to receive love…

*H*ow will I know her?

I will know her by
Her being
By her aura
Though she be
A glimpse
A flash
My eye will know

I will know her
Even if she comes
In the darkness
Of the darkest night
Her fragrance…
Will sing to me

Even if her sound
Should be a whisper
My ear will know

I will know her
Even if we
But brush past
Each other in the crowd
Her touch will call
To my brain…
She is here!

How will she know me?

If she is ready…
She will know me

I will search for you

I know that you
Will be searching too

I will watch for you
As I watch the day break
The sun set

I will listen for you
In the singing of the river
The mating of the tree branches

And if we keep our hearts open
Surely we shall pass through
The doors of loneliness
Into the warmth of love

       I watch
         I listen
            I wait…

*H*igh, high up on a hill
In a house of ruby glass
Living in the warmth
Of the sun

Lives the love I look for

In a ruby glass house
Without a door
Burning, reflecting
From the eye of my desire

At times
I hold my breath
Did I hear a sound?
Was there a signal?

I must be patient

Morning comes
When night is done

> Burn all your candles
> Light all your lamps
> Between sunset and dawn
> It is still night

Today
Time has stopped

A minute is still a minute
An hour is still an hour

And yet

The past and the future
Hang in perfect balance
All focused on the present

A sweet flow of excitement
Warms me

You are near

                              You are here

But you seem unsure

Are you ready?
Do you know me?

You seem unsure...

Do I offer too little
Or is it too much?

You seem unsure

Am I too late
Or is it too soon?...

I have known you
For a thousand years
In other times and other worlds

I have known your heart
Your mind and your very soul

We have traveled separately
Through endless space and time
To be together here

I have always known
That it would come to pass

I have watched and waited

I could enter a crowded room
And in an instant
Know that this was not
The time nor the place

And now…
Today…
I hear a sound…
And I know…
I sense your presence…
And I know…

Your questions touch me
You ask:

Will it always be easy?
Will it be forever?

I wish I could answer yes...
I can only say

Let's begin
To try
To do
To build
To breathe
To live

With patience

With care

With an open mind...

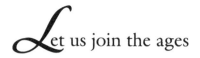
*L*et us join the ages

The tides flow
The sun rises and sets
The seasons come and go
The moon and the stars
Light the night way
For each of us

What we plant today
Will root and grow

Let us plant a seed
        Love and protect it
        Feed and warm it

Surely a tree will rise
To take its place in the sun

            Let us plant today
            The seed which will be
            The tree of us...

Yes
You are

I understand because
I am too

Each of us exists
Separate and alone

This is your Spring
Your precious time
To blossom
To be

Will you be with me?

      And now
      At last

      We are

            Side-by-side

            Together-opposed

            In spite of each other

            Because of each other…

*I*n the midst of lies
And painful sorrows
Lonely men without tomorrows
Promises not meant for keeping
Curtains drawn but not for sleeping
On top of the mountain stand
You and I...

In the rushing
      Crushing
           Pell-mell dashing
Flow of moments going by
Blowing winds and falling leaves
Swaying trees that bend and sigh
Prayers floating, hearts emoting
In the center ring stand
You and I

Move slowly

Oh so slowly

Make time stand still

I wake up to

A warm wet sunrise

Where my love lies...

I am deeply moved
By a shaft of sunlight
Breaking through the trees
By a piece of music
Drifting out of a passing car
The sandpipers on the beach
Running to and fro
Playing tag with the surf
Because of you…

I can think back on times when
I thought I saw
Thought I heard
Places I've visited
But didn't really experience

I am a child
I look forward to each new day
With a sense of adventure
There is so much to learn...
Because of you...

    Your presence
    Brings peace to my heart

    Your touch
    Is the warmth of the sun

The Tree of Us

I walk softly
Through the valley of our love
Carefully — I avoid crushing
The smallest leaf or branch
It is alive
It is precious
It is holy
All the great mysteries are resolved
All the great questions are answered

But...
The way of love
Is so fragile...

Last night...

I held you not so close to me
Being only half convinced
That you were where you wanted to be

You held me in a half sure way
Sensing my indecision

Oh my darling

Today

All day —

I thought of you

My being is broken
With pain beyond bearing

Is there anything left behind
When the sun disappears?

Is there anything left behind
When the morning dew dries?

Is there anything left behind
When words lead to tears?

Is there anything left behind
When a love dies?

For Any Pain
I Have Caused You...

For the times
When I said things
I shouldn't have
    I'm sorry

For the times
When I did things
I shouldn't have done
I ask you to
    Forgive me

I find no pleasure
In giving you pain
It makes me feel better
To make you feel good

We started with love
And when our love
Was sometimes shaken
We braced it
With understanding
To give it strength

And when our dreams
Were sometimes shattered
We picked up the pieces
And carefully put them
Together

Binding them with patience
And time…
We nursed each other
Through defeat
And learned
To be graceful
In triumph
And now

We are twice blessed
We are still lovers
And we are friends

For All Mankind

I wish for all mankind
The sweet simple joy
That we have found together

I know that it will be

And we shall celebrate
We shall taste the wine
And the fruit

Celebrate: the sunset and the sunrise
the cold and the warm
the sounds and the silences
the voices of the children

Celebrate the dreams and hopes
Which have filled the souls of
All decent men and women

We shall lift our glasses and toast
With tears of joy

*W*hen love happens
   Through a person or
   A song or a poem

What joy
   What excitement
To know that I
   All of me
My child and my adult
   All of me
Is touched again
   With the flowing love
   Of the best that is me
   And my fellow man
     That part of us…
     That cares

*I*f all the deeds of man
   Were grains of sand
And if all those grains
   Of sand were deposited
On a balance scale

   If one side of the scale
      Were the deeds
         Which ennoble humanity
   And the other side weighed
      The deeds which degrade
         The individual

         Would you not
            Count it as a blessing
            To be given the choice
            Each day
               To drop a few grains
               On the side of decency?

So this is the
  Blessed opportunity
  Provided to each of us
      Each day
    To tip the scale
    With a few small grains
    Of kindness
      With a smile
          With a word of encouragement
          A promise kept
              Or an offer of help
              At a moment of need

*M*ay you be guided by
  The heavenly light

  May your dreams
      Become solid and sound

  May your goals be
      Well chosen and surely found

  May your deeds be touched
      By decency and grace

  And above all
      May you find the time
          To be kind

When We Are Apart

— ✦ —

There is no peace
    Without harmony
No harmony
    Without music

There is no music
    Without song
No song
    Without beauty

There is no beauty
    Without laughter
No laughter
    Without joy

There is no joy
    Without kindness
No kindness
    Without caring

No caring
    Without love
No love
    Without you

I love you
Not for what
I want you to be
But for what you are

I loved you then
For what you were
I love you now
For what you have become

I miss you
And not only you

I miss what I am
When you are here...

*I*n the desert
     I learned about heat

In the snow
     I learned about cold

When you left
     I learned about lonely

If I were to take the time
To tell you about each time
That I think of you
    I would spend
    All my time
    Telling you about
        Thinking of you

I want to see you again
To hold your hand
To touch your face
To feel the earth stand still again
I want to breathe with you
As one again
Not just now and then
But always

*S*weet is
　　The sunbreak
　　After the rain

Welcome is
　　The breeze
　　That follows the heat

Warm is
　　The fire
　　Against the snow

Yet none
　　So precious
　　As your smile
That says

　　Welcome home...

　　After we've
　　　　Been apart

Will I Think of You?

Will I think of you?

Only at sunrise
      Which is God's beginning

For you were there
      At the beginning of me

When I came alive
      And discovered my place

My worth
      The beauty of earth

And the miracle of daybreak
      Once again

And the richness of mornings
      To come

Only in the morning

Each time
   The darkness of past
Is chased
   By the light of now

      Will I think of you...

      Only then

Only at night
        Where the silence

And the blackness
        Is touched occasionally
By a lonely cat
        Or suspicious puppy
A passing plane
        Red eye winking
To the stars
        Who refuse to be seduced
When I hear
        Your whispered love
                In the tree rustle
When I feel your secret hand
        Exploring me
                Drifting across my skin
To rest in a friendly
        Harbor

        And my mind tells me
                I am alone

        But my heart knows better

        Only then

                Will I think

                        Of you

*W*ill I think of you?

Only when it snows

>And the whiteness
>The pure
>>Virgin
>>>Whiteness

Covers the face
>Of the earth
>To cleanse the trampled
>>Corruption
>>>Of times past

Like a new love
>Delicate

Untracked
>Unexplored

Waiting for the lovers
>To choose carefully
>The path to heaven
>>Together

When I am overcome by
      The realization that you
      Created the whiteness and the
                Purity

And you led me
      Like a child
          Both of us children

Into
      A new and pure

      Wonderful land of our own

Where each step
      Left a priceless
         Landmark

And promised a new
Place to explore
A new step to come

      Then I will
         Watch the snow
      Falling in swirls and flurries
      Of perfect crystal tears

I will watch
The new virginity
      Embrace the earth
         And I will think of you

*O*nly when it rains

I will recall
    An aching soul and a crying heart
    Standing in pools of the saddest light

Back to back
    And moving away
And I knew
    The tears in your heart
Would soon be on your cheeks

    To wet my fingers
    As I held your face
    Up to the light
    To remember
    For tomorrow

Then…

    Whenever the eyes of heaven
    Overflow
    And God's tears
    Wash across my window
    I shall see again
    Those streaks of love
    Which flowed for me
    To bind an aching soul
    To a crying heart

        And I will think of you

And when the day is clear

    After a rain
    And a new vision
Of the landscape
    Is visible to all
      Who will
        Bother to look and see

        When I remember how I felt
        Safe enough with you
          To let you see me
          Cry

When the tears washed clean
The windows of my vision
And I could see
    The past and present of myself
    And find hope and strength
For the future

      And after the rain of my crying
        I felt washed
        And fresh and loved
        As my babyself
        Must have felt

      When my mother
        Bathed her infant

      Then after each rain
        How can I help
          But think of you?

*W*ill I think of you?

Only when it's cold
And I'm shivering
Against the wind

And suddenly from inside
The core of me
From my deepest depths
Comes
A small warming flame
Which wants to grow
And I fight it
Until I realize I need it

Want it
To flow through me

To fill me
Because
It is you

Only in the spring

When the first warm breezes of April
Give courage
	To the youngest
		Tenderest
Shoots of nature
		To appear
			To live
				To grow

When the thaw
		In the mountains
Sends the pure cold
		Cascading
			Waters
Down the
	Hillside
		To fill the streams

As you fill me
		To laughter
			And tears

			Only then...

			Will I think of you

*W*ill I think of you?

    Only when I feel
      Warmed and wanted

Though once
    I felt I was outside
    Looking in
    Disconnected
Watching the world
    Go by

        Then…

    I'll remember
      That in your love
      I found acceptance

    And I'll think of you

        Only when I laugh

          At a joke of others
          Or my own

          Or a memory of you

        And the laughter rises
          Out of the well of me

        To be tasted
          By my mouth and lips

When the tickle rolls
   Through my body

To remind me
   Of days and nights
Of free laughter with you

   Even while others stared
At the crazy couple
   Wondering what could be so funny
In a world
   Of grim rushing

         And painful waiting

Urgent hoping
   And sad silences

      Then
         When the laughter
      Is multiplied
         By past joys remembered
      And I can't stop
      Even to catch my breath
         Or to give relief to my aching sides

         I'll realize
            That the laughter of my life
      Is for you
         Because of you

And I'll think of you

         But only then

*O*r when I'm sad and lost
　　Tired of trying

When the tears and pains
　　Of the world
All seem to be mine

When there is no one but you
Who would really understand
The emptiness of my soul
　　The sorrow
Of trying
　　And failing

Of knowing that
　　Life can be a trial
　　Where the judge and jury
Sometimes sit
With faces of stone
　And will not respond
　Even to a cry
　From the truest heart

　　　When I know
　　That the final precious blossom
　　Clinging to the tree
　　　Will surely fall
　　　Under the constant
　　　　Persistent
　　Pressing of the wind

When I know that you
And only you
    Could see all this
    And hear all this
And be with me in my sadness
In silent understanding

And shed tears
    For my sorrow

Then I will think of you

Only when the turn of fortune
    Comes my way again

    When I ride
    The crest of triumph
    Glowing with pride
    In the promise fulfilled

    When the adoring crowd
    Has returned
    With shouts of approval

        Then I will search their faces
        Looking for the one
        Who stood beside me
        In defeat
        And should be there
        In the victory
        Which is empty
            Without you

*W*ill I think of you?

    No…

  Only when I'm with others

  Surrounded
    In a crowded party room
Listening to
    Several conversations

People communicating
    Or trying to…

Watching the
    Blur of figures and
Faces go past
    None coming into focus

Except yours

  Again and again
In each corner
In each chair
    In every smile

Only you
    Persistent
        Forever

           Only then

Will I think of you?

    Only on the highway
        When I travel
    Searching for money and fame
    And finding that neither feeds me

When I pass
    The other travelers
        Some going my way
    And some not

    But I realize
That this is what we all
Must do...

    To fall behind
    The traveling flow
        And catch up
    And pass others
        Then fall behind again
    Passed by those
        Who rush on
    Believing that
        It is best
To be there first

    But I know that this is
Where we all are

        On the highway

        That there is no "here" or "there"...
      There is only
        The coming and going

If we can help
One
Who finds the way
Too hard or too long
    Then that is worth
    All of being
And I will try to help

    Because someone helped me

Someone who cared more
About the brothers on the
Road
    Than about the
        Gifts at the end
And that someone was you

    So I will think of you

Only on the beach
    Where the timeless
        Never-ending surge
    Of water
        Changes
    The face of earth
        Again and again
    Each minute of the day
            Night
            And always

Where the children
And the aged
Come together
To chase a wave
The surf
Of a dream

Where the tide shifts constantly
Teaching me
    That today is only today
And whatever I have
                Good or bad
                Much or little
    Must change
                Or it will rot
                And die

Then and there when I recall
The change
    In this thing called me
The new sides
    New forms
        New shapes of me

Which came
        When you
        Washed across
My being

Then, there
        On the beach
                I will think

                Of you

$\mathcal{W}$ill I think of you?

Only when I'm alone

Staring out my window

Into space…

       Which becomes you

Your love
Smiling back
   To the warmth
     Of my heart

Filling the emptiness
        The loneliness
            With your being

Only then

    Will I think of you

Only when I hear music

And the songs
Of the poet singers
Remind me
That

All things are for all
People
That there is
A love and a sorrow
A joy and a pain
Which each of us separately
Feels
As if it is ours alone

And it is only ours
Even while it is everyone's

For each of us is
A separate miracle
In a collective miracle

Brought together
For a moment
By a group of notes
And a scan of words

From the heart
Of one
Who dares
To think

That others
Might feel
As he feels

And he sings it out to us
　　As a gift

To be accepted
　　　Or rejected

　　　　But given with
　　　　　A heart of love

I thank them
　　The poet singers

Who give us communion

And help us join with
　　Each other
　　　　Think of each other

And bless us
　　With each other's love

　　　　For in that music—love—rhythm

　　　　I feel your
　　　　　Heart beat

And I will think of you

Will I think of you?

Only when we're apart
And the aching joy-pain of our love
Surrounds me
    Filling the air I breathe

Only with each blink of my
    Eye which yearns
    To re-open to find you here
    With me

Only with each clock-tick
Which makes my ear perk up
Hopeful
    That it has heard
    Your key in the door

Only when I daydream and re-dream
Our coming together again

When the world will fall away
    Leaving only two figures

            Yours and mine

Merged into
    A classic chord

            Loving…

                Being loved
                    In each
                        Part of harmony

*O*nly on special days

Birthdays, holidays

And other days…

When those who
Give to each other
And live for each other

Travel
For hours or days
Or for an instant

To hold
Or dream-hold
Each other

To exchange
Heart-warmth
And body-warmth

When we commemorate

And celebrate

The special days
Of a life of love

Then and especially then

Because the day is special
As your glorious being
Is special
I will think of you

Only when we're together

And I can think of nothing else
And everything else
Because we together
Are everything
And our togetherness is
All things

Then as always
And forever
I will think of you

In the Garden of My Life

I have a garden that I love
Once in a while it looks perfect
All the watering, feeding, pruning and love
   add up to a moment of beauty

Then I think…
   if only I could keep it this way
     preserve this moment forever
But my garden is alive
Time and seasons bring changes
Living things must change

A life is like a garden
Perfect moments can be had
   but not preserved
     except in memory
I am a living thing that must change
If I can accept the changes
   I can accept myself
And when I accept myself
   I can enjoy the changes
     and the beauty of the changes
       in the garden of my life

I have lived with me
   for a long time
      and plan to continue

I would like
   to keep my friendship
      with others

But
   I must keep faith
      with myself

*B*ecause
      I have known despair
      I value hope

   Because
      I have tasted frustration
      I value fulfillment

   Because
      I have been lonely
      I value love

I have learned again
    To trust myself

Sometimes…
    It isn't easy

Sometimes…
    Someone who seems
        to know
    Someone who seems
        to be wiser
    Can convince me
        that I'm on
        the wrong path

Not wanting to seem
        too stubborn
Not wanting to be
        too difficult
        and above all
        wanting to be
            liked…

I have occasionally
    been persuaded
        to leave my own path
            to go the way of another
        even when all my instincts
            tell me to trust myself

                Sometimes it works
                    but often it doesn't

And worst of all…

    Sometimes it's hard
        to find my own way again

*W*hen I truly give
In a love
As the artist gives
In his art
I am fulfilled
Manyfold

A Precious Lesson

There is a great pleasure
   In wanting

The object of desire
      Seems so perfect
      So useful
      So necessary
You wonder how you
      Ever got along without it
And you know that you must
      Have it now

      Closets full of neglected
         Once-desired objects
      Tell me that
            It was the wanting
            That was important

      I have learned
            A precious lesson

      I have learned
            To want
               What I have

I am not immortal

Whatever I put off for later
May never be

Whoever doesn't know now
That I love them
May never know

I have killed time
      I have squandered it
            I have lost days… weeks…
As a man of unlimited wealth
Might drop coins on the street
And never look back
I know now that there will be an end
A limit
      But there is time
      Valuable and precious time
      To walk
         Talk
           Breathe
     Time to touch
        Taste
          Care
    To warm the child
    Who is cold and lonely
    There is time to love
    I promise myself…
         I will

I Guess I'm Just an Old-Fashioned Spaceman

Rocket ships
Are exciting
But so are roses
On a birthday

Computers are exciting
But so is a sunset

And logic
Will never replace
Love

Sometimes I wonder
Where I belong
In the future
Or
In the past

I guess I'm just
An old-fashioned
Spaceman